INSIDE...

Published 2019.
Little Brother Books, Ground Floor, 23 Southernhay East, Exeter, Devon, EX1 1QL
Printed in Poland.
books@littlebrotherbooks.co.uk | www.littlebrotherbooks.co.uk

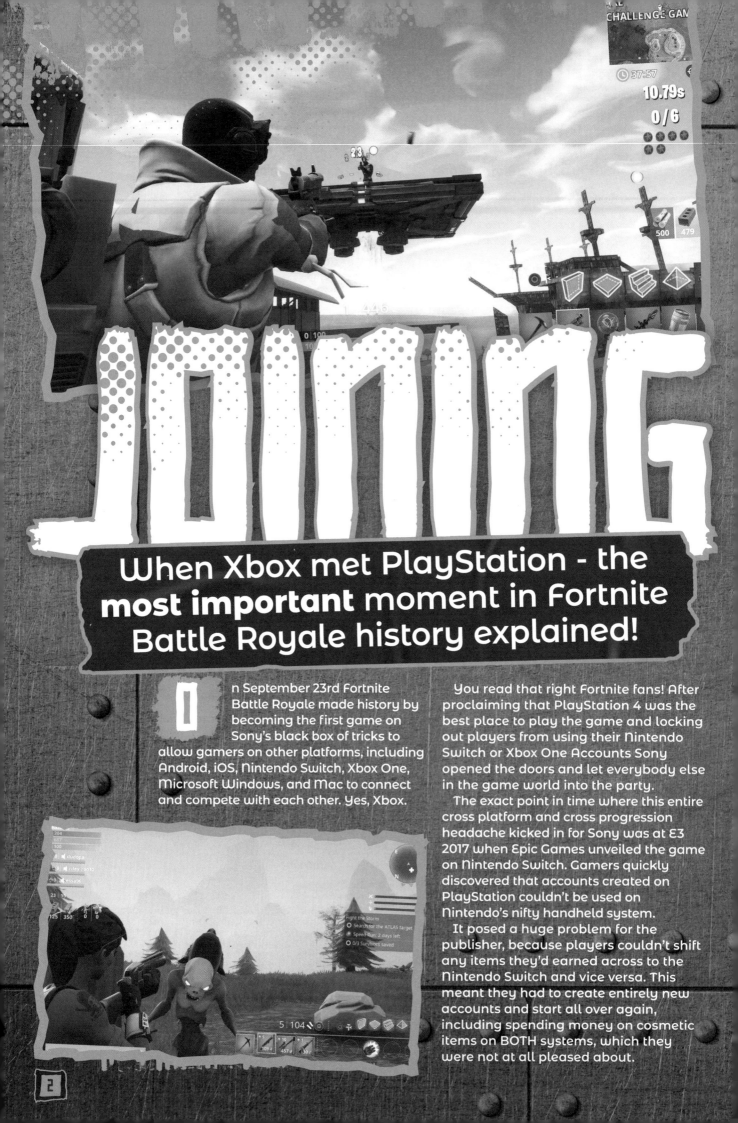

JOINING

When Xbox met PlayStation - the **most important** moment in Fortnite Battle Royale history explained!

On September 23rd Fortnite Battle Royale made history by becoming the first game on Sony's black box of tricks to allow gamers on other platforms, including Android, iOS, Nintendo Switch, Xbox One, Microsoft Windows, and Mac to connect and compete with each other. Yes, Xbox.

You read that right Fortnite fans! After proclaiming that PlayStation 4 was the best place to play the game and locking out players from using their Nintendo Switch or Xbox One Accounts Sony opened the doors and let everybody else in the game world into the party.

The exact point in time where this entire cross platform and cross progression headache kicked in for Sony was at E3 2017 when Epic Games unveiled the game on Nintendo Switch. Gamers quickly discovered that accounts created on PlayStation couldn't be used on Nintendo's nifty handheld system.

It posed a huge problem for the publisher, because players couldn't shift any items they'd earned across to the Nintendo Switch and vice versa. This meant they had to create entirely new accounts and start all over again, including spending money on cosmetic items on BOTH systems, which they were not at all pleased about.

Those last four words - select third party content - are vitally important to gamers the world over. Why? Because it sounds like Fortnite may have just opened the floodgates for a whole host of games to be added to the cross platform roster.

Imagine a world where you can play FIFA, Call of Duty, Battlefield, Street Fighter or WWE with friends on Nintendo Switch, Xbox One, Microsoft Windows, and Mac? That would

FORCES

By locking players out it looked bad for Sony and for PlayStation, so it was a huge relief to fans of Fortnite Battle Royale that the publisher and developer lifted the ban and sent the game world into a tailspin. This is a huge deal for players, and not just of Fortnite Battle Royale. But before we talk about why, it's important to note that it was Epic Games' behemoth title that was no doubt solely responsible for this new shift in policy.

It's arguably the most popular game in the world, and it was quite clear that the unique progression mechanics and in-game purchases were what forced Sony to change its mind and allow gamers to share. In announcing the new feature Sony stated that, "Following a comprehensive evaluation process, SIE has identified a path toward supporting cross-platform features for select third party content."

be awesome! Epic Games is busy working on an Account Merge feature, which would allow Fortnite players with multiple console-linked accounts to transfer Battle Royale purchases, records, V-Bucks, and Save the World campaign access. However, due to some teething problems the feature hasn't been released at the time of going to press. Here's hoping that the developer resolves these very soon! Either way, the future is bright for cross-platform play between PlayStation 4 owners and gamers the world over!

STAY FROSTY

Diving into the ice cool Fortnite Deep Freeze bundle.

In late 2018 Epic Games and Warner Bros. Interactive teamed up to release a super cool Fortnite exclusive console edition on PlayStation 4, Xbox One and Nintendo Switch. The bundle, which hit retail shelves across the nation back in November, included a whole heap of goodies for players and will set you back £24.99 on all three formats at the time of going to press.

The box includes an install of Fortnite Battle Royale if you haven't already got it downloaded onto your machine. It does not include a copy of Fortnite Save The World, which will cost you extra. At the time of going to press The Standard Founders Pack costs between £32.99 and £34.99 on PlayStation Store and Xbox Games Store, whereas the Deluxe edition costs £49.99 on both game stores.

DEEP FREEZE BUNDLE CONTAINS

FORTNITE BATTLE ROYALE GAME

FROSTBITE SKIN + CHILL-AXE

COLD FRONT GLIDER

FREEZING POINT BACK BLING

1,000 V-BUCKS

Next up is 1000 V-Bucks, more than enough to cover a single Battle Pass. The Battle Passes are released at the start of every season in Fortnite Battle Royale, and work on two tiers - silver and gold, with silver being free and gold requiring you to purchase the Battle Pass at the start of each new season for 950 V-Bucks.

Alongside the V-Bucks and the install of Fortnite Battle Royale there is also a Legendary Skin called Frostbit, which also features the Freezing Point Back Bling, Cold Front Glider and Chill-Axe Harvesting Tool. It's a slick set and ideal for anyone looking to jump into Fortnite Battle Royale for the first time, especially with the addition of the V-Bucks, which allows you to purchase a Battle Pass.

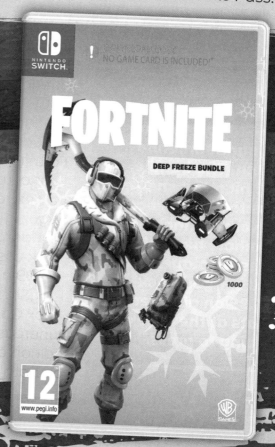

The Deep Freeze bundle is available on store shelves now, but if you don't feel like taking a walk to shops you can purchase it via the PlayStation, Nintendo and Xbox Game Stores. However, if you are playing Fortnite Save The World it's worth noting that items in the Deep Freeze Bundle are not cross transferable.

Animal Antics

Meet the cuddly, cute and **scary Pets** of Fortnite Battle Royale!

Ever wanted to drop into a Fortnite Battle Royale match with a dog or dragon strapped to your back? Well now you can with the Fortnite Pets Back Bling! These cuddly critters were rumoured to be appearing in the game for a while, so it was a huge deal for fans of the game when they launched back in September 2018. It meant Players could dive into battle on the Fortnite Island with an animal on their back ready to kick some serious butt, and look super cool doing it!

Furry Back Bling

Fortnite Pets are Back Bling, so that means they're unlocked and equipped in Fortnite Battle Royale like any other Back Bling or character dressing. Of course the difference here is that these cuddly little rascals actually react to what's going on around you during a match. The Pets were included with the Season Six Battle Pass, and each one came with a selection of colours the further along you progressed.

Own 'Em All!

Owners of the Season Six Battle Pass really had to work to earn

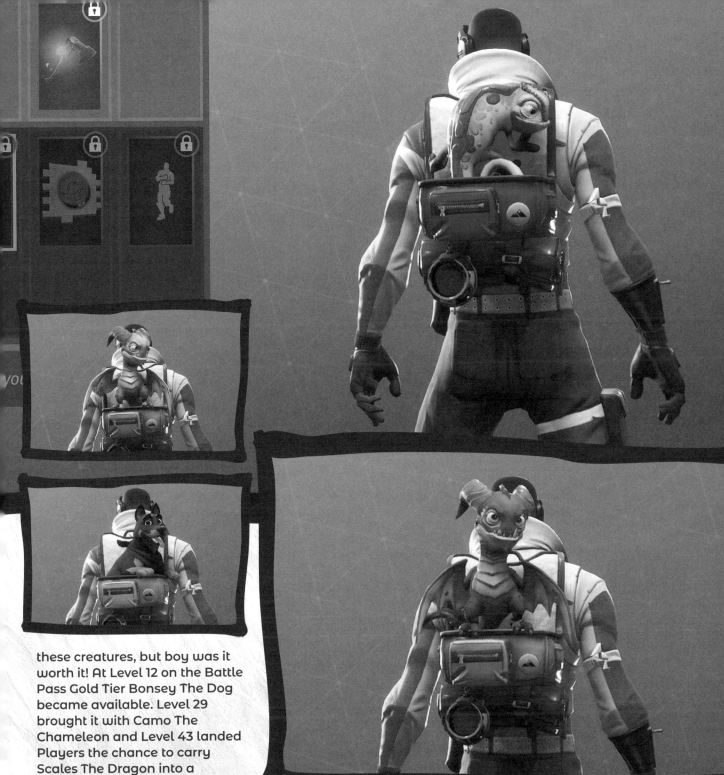

these creatures, but boy was it worth it! At Level 12 on the Battle Pass Gold Tier Bonsey The Dog became available. Level 29 brought it with Camo The Chameleon and Level 43 landed Players the chance to carry Scales The Dragon into a 100-player brawl. As Players progressed through the Season Six Battle Pass by completing challenges additional colours became available, including a black Scales The Dragon and a Mocha Bonesy The Dog.

What Do They Do?!

They do absolutely nothing, Fortnite fans! The Pets are simply nothing more than cosmetic items exactly like other Back Bling that can be unlocked or purchased in the game. Cosmetic items such as these have no impact on the game; they're simply a style choice, and a way to jazz up your character's look in battle. But who cares, because they're cuddly pets and they look really awesome, people!

Safe And Sound

One of the biggest concerns Fortnite fans had when the Pets were announced was what exactly happened to these cute animals when an opposing player knocked them out of a match. We're here to tell you that all is well – the Pets simply spend a moment or two looking around, wondering what happened and then simply disappear into the ether until you bring them back for another match!

WILD, WILD, WEST

Take a trip back in time with Fortnite Battle Royale's new Limited Time Mode!

"This town ain't big enough for the hundred of us!" so said the patched notes for his cowboy flavoured slice of action that Epic Games rolled out right around the time Rockstar Games' Red Dead Redemption was breaking sales records on PlayStation 4 and Xbox One consoles.

The developers were smart enough to realise the hoopla that would surround the launch of one the biggest games of the year and in order to ensure Fortnite fans stayed put, they cooked up this western Limited Time Mode, and boy is it a heck of a lot of fun to play around with! ●

Kaboom!

One of the biggest additions to the game with the Wild West Limited Time Mode is Dynamite. It packs one hell of a bang, dealing out 70 damage points if it hits another player, and 800 damage points to structures. That means, if you're hiding out in a self-made structure and someone's hurling Dynamite your way you'd better bail out of there as quickly as possible, because it's coming down!

Nice Shootin' Tex

Considering this Limited Time Mode is set in Frontier Times it's only fitting that some of the more modern and futuristic weaponry is culled whenever you dive in. The only guns you'll wield throughout a match are Hunting Rifles, Pump Shotguns, Double Barrel Shotguns, Six Shooters and, on occasion, the awesome Mini-gun. With weapons like this it means you're going to have to get up close and personal the majority of the time, so you'd better be sure of two things – one: you're a damn good shot, and two: you keep that weapon loaded at all times!

Drink Up, Cowboy!

Shield Potions are an essential gameplay component in Fortnite Battle Royale, but in Wild West Limited Time Mode they've been cut too, and instead you're left to dash around the map hunting down containers of Slurp Juice to refill defences. Remember, Slurp Juice takes a little time to get down the hatch, so watch your back while you chug one of those bad boys!

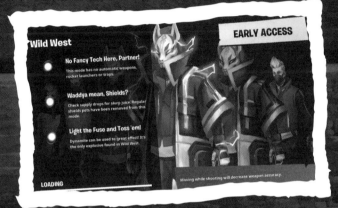

Cozy Campfire

Another way to heal up during battle is with the addition of Cozy Campfires. They are extremely useful in battle, because they don't just heal you, they also heal teammates, so if you have one and your squad is running low on health drop it in!

SAVING THE WORLD AIN'T FREE

Fortnite **Save The World** free-to-play has been delayed. Let's find out why!

Before we get into the reasons why Fortnite Save The World is not currently free (despite Epic Games telling fans this would be the case in 2018) on consoles and PC, let's take a look at how it works in comparison to Fortnite's Battle Royale mode, as well as what you get for your hard earned money if you do decide to go ahead and pay for it, before it goes free-to-play sometime in 2019.

What is save the world?

It was released in July of 2017 and is a co-operative play survival game where you team up with three other players to battle waves of zombie-like enemies. It's got pretty much all the ingredients that make the Battle Royale mode so great, including shooting and building, as well as elements of tower defence. It was created and developed by Epic Games and People Can Fly, the team behind Bulletstorm and Gears of War: Judgement.

There are multiple versions of the game, including the Standard edition, Deluxe Edition, Super Deluxe Edition and Limited Edition. Prices vary from platform to platform, but keep an eye out for discounts because Epic is always slashing the price to encourage new players to join the fight against the marauding zombies!

When will it be free?

Anyway, onto the big, burning question – when will it be free to all players like Fortnite Battle Royale? Right now, dates are hazy, but Epic Games is working on a whole host of features for it in order to ensure the transition is smooth and simple. Here's what the team said back in late 2018 when it decided to hold off on releasing the new model of Fortnite Save The World.

"We're working on a broad set of features, reworks, and backend system scaling we believe are needed to go free-to-play. 'Save the World' has grown consistently since our launch in July 2017 and Fortnite overall has experienced unprecedented growth. Scaling up for the legions of player heroes who will be joining the fight is key to providing an excellent experience. This applies to all of our players, old and new, so we're taking the time to get this right."

Here's hoping the team get these features in place relatively quickly so Fortnite fans the world over can start enjoying this very cool mode – FOR FREE! ●

SMASH!

Everything you need to know about Quadcrashers in Fortnite Battle Royale!

The team at Epic Games are always adding new and fun stuff to Fortnite Battle Royale, and Quadcrashers are arguably one of the most enjoyable vehicle additions to the game so far. They're fast, furious and can bust through just about anything when hit with at high speed. To really master these new machines you need to know how they work on the battlefield, so let's take a look at them.

Jump on!

Quadcrashers can seat up to two players at a time, so if you're playing Duos and grab one of these be sure to honk the horn to get your teammates' attention so they can jump aboard and ride with you to different areas of the map.

Parking Spots

You can find Quadcrashers all over the map. Locations include Risky Reels, Retail Row, Salty Springs and Greasy Grove. And this is just a small selection of spots they're dotted around. Chances are wherever you go you'll find one!

Race Day!

If you feel like trying something other than shooting people grab yourself a Quadcrasher and head to the east of Junk Junction where you'll find a racetrack, which lets you compete in timed races using the newly created vehicles. Vroom!

Engine Problems

Quadcrashers are LOUD so don't barrel into the middle of a chaotic shootout between other players, because they will hear you coming a mile away and blast you to kingdom come. Either ditch the vehicle or boost it as fast as you can!

Hit 'n' Run

The Quadcrashers are designed to smash through structures thanks to their heavy-duty construction, so use them to burst across the battlefield and smash down enemies in structures, or to ram through walls to take out players on the other side.

Rough Landing

Quadcrashers may be tough, but that doesn't mean they'll protect you if you do something daft like speed off the edge of a cliff and land awkwardly at the bottom. Doing that will result in your character taking damage, so be careful!

Air Time

Like the ATV in previous updates, one of the most enjoyable things to do with the Quadcrasher is to build ramps and boost off them to catch some serious air. Just make sure you nail that landing or it's going to sting, folks – a hell of a lot!

Flyboy

Ever wanted to see what another player looks like soaring through the air? Then grab yourself a Quadcrasher, hit the boost button and find some enemies on the battlefield. Once you hit them the vehicle will send them flying sky high!

SLICK SKINS!

There are so many great skins to choose from in Fortnite Battle Royale it's impossible to list every single one of them here. If we wanted to do that it would probably take an entire book! That said, some skins are just so cool they need to be added to your collection, so without further ado we've put together a collection of some of the best ones that have appeared on the Fortnite Battle Royale Store to date. Just remember, skins cost money so choose wisely before spending your hard earned pocket money on deciding which one fits your avatar best!

Patch Patroller

If you like spooky skins then you'll want to grab this Patch Patroller that was released as part of a Halloween themed pack in 2018. A masked vigilante in a black and orange getup, this guy is guaranteed to strike fear into your opponents!

Jack Gourdon

Clearly a bit of a nod to The Nightmare Before Christmas, Jack Gourdon comes clad in a black tux covered in a series of Halloween lanterns. He's both stylish and spooky in equal measure, making him one of our favourite new skins out there.

Deadfire

The Wild West comes to Fortnite Battle Royale with Deadfire, a seriously cool cowboy kitted out in slick duster, cowboy hat and the Shackled Stone Back Bling that causes the character to emit spectral flames after a certain number of kills.

Brainiac

No, it's not the villain from Superman (but it could be!). This uncommon skin features a soldier with strange green skin, an army vest and red neck scarf. Released right before the annual Halloween event, many believe he's a zombie!

Hay Man

Eek! If you see this terrifying skin coming at you wielding a gun you'd better run! Hay Man is designed to look like a scarecrow come to life, and boy it works! He's got glowing red eyes, bird skull necklace and bird's nest as his Back Bling.

Valkyrie

This Legendary female skin is one of the most awesome to appear in the game so far. Culled from the world of Norse mythology, Valkyrie comes kitted out in reinforced steel, spiked helmet and glowing eyes that burn with bright blue flames.

NightShade

Be mysterious. Be a Tomatohead! This slick chick comes clad in an all-black suit that closely resembles outfits we've seen before such as cover field agents and assassins. She's part of the Pizza Pit set that included a delivery bag and pizza cutter.

Stage Slayer

It's Slash from Guns 'N' Roses! Actually, no it isn't, but we're pretty certain the team at Epic were thinking of him when they designed this new skin that features a rock star in top hat and black sunglasses, and is part of the Garage Band set.

Wukong

Inspired by Monkey King, one of the greatest ever stories from Chinese mythology, Wukong comes dressed in mighty Chinese-styled armour and is part of the Wukong set that includes the Jingu Bang Harvesting Tool and Royale Flags.

Sushi Master

Do you like sushi with your guns? We do! Sushi Master is a Rare skin that comes with an avatar dressed as a traditional Japanese Sushi Chef. The cool thing about this skin is that if you snag it you unlock the Chef's Choice Back Bling.

Overtaker

Now this is definitely one of the coolest costumes we've seen in recent updates. Just look at this guy in his white racing jacket, trousers and racing helmet. Once you nab this skin you can grab the Lane Splitter Back Bling with samurai sword!

The Ace

Part of the sticky fingered Getaway Gang set, but only available to anyone who purchased the Fortnite Battle Royale Start Pack #3 at the time of going to press, The Ace comes with the Cuff Case Back Bling and Crowbar Harvesting Tool.

Beef Boss

Part of the Durr Burger Set, Beef Boss is terrifying thanks to his hamburger head and weirdly long tongue! We know it's part of a Halloween Set, but if we saw this on the battlefield it'd send us running off in the opposite direction. Scary stuff!

Sun Tan Specialist

Time to hit the beach with Sun Tan Specialist, a hip looking lifeguard complete with shorts, flip flops, sunglasses, suntan lotion and, if you want to complete the outfit, the Rescue Ring Back Bling. He's the perfect reminder of how much we love summer!

Wreck Raider

The Wreck Raider is an Epic skin clad in full scuba gear, and despite the fact he's wearing flippers he moves around the map just fine in Fortnite Battle Royale. Now, be warned – this skin DOES NOT allow you to swim underwater just in case you had any ideas!

Vertex

Vertex is badass, and definitely one of the more striking skins to choose from on the Fortnite Battle Royale Store. Featuring full-body armour, helmet and the Deflector Back Bling, Vertex is part of the Apex Protocol Set released last year.

Dusk

Dusk is a really cool, villainous character that came as part of the Nite Coven Set during Season 6 of Fortnite Battle Royale. She sported wicked looking blood red eyes and white hair, and you could also kit her out with Dusk Wings Back Bling.

Giddy-Up

This weird and whacky outfit featured a character riding a Loot Llama. Yes, really! It also had a pair of fake legs, which looked completely bonkers and will have your opponents in stitches right before you blast them into oblivion for the win!

DJ Yonder

Pump up the volume on the battlefield with DJ Yonder, an epic skin released alongside the Season 6 Battle Pass. This cool dude comes in a green suit and a zany mask shaped like a robot llama that reflects light just like a disco ball.

Bunnymoon

Bunnymoon is an uncommon female skin that features a slick character clad in a purple and black striped top with combat pants wrapped up in what look like Christmas tree lights. She didn't come with any bonus items, but she's still cool!

Spider Knight

Whoa! Spider Knight is one scary skin that's for sure, and we certainly wouldn't want to meet this guy on the battlefield in the dark of night. Clad in a spooky spider themed helmet with leather jacket and dagger, he came as part of the Arachnid set.

Arachne

Also arriving as part of the Arachnid set, Arachne arrived during the Halloween season of 2018 sporting a black and leather vest, super skinny leather trousers, gauntlets and one of the coolest looking helmets in the game. Oh, and spider Back Bling!

Airheart

Released as part of the Aviation set that included the Exhaust skydiving trail and Dirigible glider skin, this red haired female character was clearly a nod to the legendary aviation pioneer, Amelia Earhart. To complete the set you could also grab the Airflow Back Bling.

Grill Sergeant

Part of the Durr Burger set, the Grill Sergeant came kitted out in a fast food employee garb that included a hat and apron. One of the funniest items he came equipped with if you went for the complete getup was the Patty Whacker Harvesting Tool.

Sanctum

Sanctum wants to suck your blood! Well, at least we think that's what this creepy vampire themed skin is thinking with his red eyes, huge claws and pale white skin! Part of the Nite Coven set alongside Dusk, Sanctum hit the Fortnite Store just in time for Halloween 2018.

ROYAL RUMBLE

It's all out war in Fortnite Battle Royale's **Team Rumble** Limited Time Mode!

The team at Epic Games sure do know how to treat their fans. They're constantly cooking up wild and whacky modes to keep players engaged should they feel like taking a break from the usual Battle Royale Mode. Enter Team Rumble Limited Time Mode, introduced in Fortnite 6.31 released back in November 2018. This kick-ass new way to play ramps up the action tenfold, and is far more aggressive than the Game Modes you're more accustomed to in Fortnite Battle Royale.

Attack, Attack, Attack!

Team Rumble Limited Time Mode is incredibly fast-paced, pitting two teams of 20 players against each other. The goal is simple; players need to work with teammates to wrack up 100 kills to win the match and grab that Victory Royale. Essentially this is a race; a race with guns, bombs and anything else that comes to hand as you wade through waves of enemies vying to take you down for a point.

Re-Animated

One of the great things about Team Rumble Limited Time Mode is that players respawn once eliminated during a match. It takes just five seconds for you to wind up back on the battlefield, so you're unlikely to miss out on much of the action. But remember, if a member of the opposing team takes you

out they're awarded a point. If that team reaches max points it means game over, Fortnite fan!

Inventory Bonuses

Another difference between this Limited Time Mode and the other Game Modes in Fortnite Battle Royale is that if you're eliminated you get to keep everything in your inventory. That way you're not wasting time running around looking for weapons once you respawn on the map. If you're the one doing the eliminating the Players you wipe out will spawn everything from ammo to building materials.

KaBlam!

Uncommon weapons and

weapons of a higher rarity spawn more frequently in Team Rumble Limited Time Mode too. These dish out a substantial amount of damage, which means you're likely to notch quite a few kills if you can master 'em. The better weaponry also encourages Players to be a little more daring; don't be afraid to barrel in there and hunt down opposing players for team points! But don't get too cocky, because it's important to stick with your team to work together if you want to nab that all-important Victory Royale. Being a Lone Wolf can be pretty dangerous in this hectic Game Mode, so watch yourself out there! ●

POP, POP, POP!

Balloon 101

Balloons are an Epic Rarity, and come in packs of 20. Six can be inflated at a time using Primary and Secondary Fire Buttons to inflate and release them. Each balloon only stays inflated for a certain amount of time, so remember that!

Everything you need to know about Balloons, the new and super exciting mode of transport in Fortnite Battle Royale!

There are so many ways of getting around in Fortnite Battle Royale, including vehicles and Gliders, but here's one we DID NOT expect to arrive in an update back in November 2018 – Balloons! Despite what you might think Balloons are extremely versatile and can be used in a variety of ways to gain the lead on the battlefield. Here are some tips and tricks to help you master them in the game.

Where To Find Them

Even though Balloons are labelled as an Epic Rarity class they're actually pretty easy to find. Packs of them are dotted around the map as Ground Loot, and they're also hidden inside Loot Chests as well as Supply Drops and Loot Llamas.

Silent & Deadly

Balloons are the only way of getting around silently in Fortnite Battle Royale. If you find a pack during a match you can use them to float into the air and sneak up on enemy structures, or infiltrate heavily populated buildings via the rooftops.

How High?

While you may be tempted to inflate Balloons and float your way to the clouds we would suggest erring on the side of caution – once you've reached a certain height they'll pop and send you plummeting to the ground. So be careful, folks!

Shoot 'Em!

If you're on the ground and spot an opponent sailing through the skies using Balloons you can shoot them. If they don't have any replacement ones you'll snag yourself a kill, but don't forget that players can do the same thing to you!

Up & Down

To increase the speed of Balloon ascension all you have to do is inflate more until you've reached your max amount. To drop down steadily to an area on the battlefield simply let go of the Balloons and sail down comfortably to the ground.

Keep Count!

When using Balloons in Fortnite Battle Royale it's definitely worth keeping an eye on how many you have in your inventory. If you're flying too high they will pop, so if you don't have enough left you're likely to fall to the ground and get eliminated.

No Weapons

One of the most important things to remember when using Balloons is that you are extremely vulnerable up there in the air and can't use a weapon, because the Primary and Secondary Fire Buttons are used for controlling ascent and descent.

THE BIG BANG

Ditch bullets for bombs in Fortnite Battle Royale's **High Explosives** Limited Time mode!

If you thought standard Fortnite Battle Royale matches were wild, then wait until you get a load of High Explosives Limited Time Mode! Brawls are still 100 player battles, but the twist here is that anything bullet related has been stripped away, and all that remains are things that go BOOM on the crazy Fortnite Island. That means you'll be grabbing rocket launchers, grenade launchers, remote explosives as well as dynamite at loot drops, and using them to down opponents.

Loot Drops

One of the great things about this Limited Time Mode is that Loot Drops are far more frequent, so be sure to keep an eye out for them as they appear in the sky. Once you spot one, be

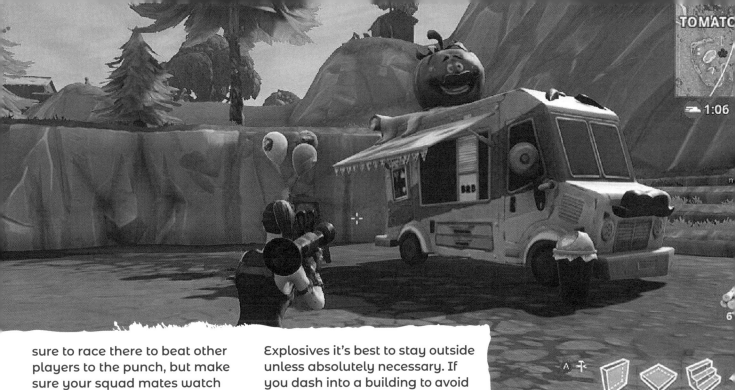

sure to race there to beat other players to the punch, but make sure your squad mates watch your back or it's game over for you! It's also important to remember that those of you prone to headshots with high-powered sniper rifles need to change up your play style. High Explosives is all about shooting from the hip. Don't waste time lining up a shot or you'll die – fast!

Stay Outside

Given that explosives are the primary weapons in High

Explosives it's best to stay outside unless absolutely necessary. If you dash into a building to avoid another player the chances are they'll lob a grenade or dynamite your way and if you're caught in the blast radius you'll be taken out. You can use staircases and walls to your advantage, but be prepared to take some damage when anything goes bang!

Jump Around

Just like in the standard Battle Royale Mode one of the most effective ways to avoid getting blown to smithereens is by leaping around the map, especially when facing down another player. Yes, it makes it that bit harder to pull off the perfect shot and take out an opponent, but bouncing around will help you avoid taking a rocket to the face.

Sneaky, Sneaky

A really effective way of taking out enemies in High Explosives Limited Time Mode is by planting remote explosives in areas containing Loot Chests, then finding a good spot to hide before waiting for a player to arrive on scene. Once they do hit that detonator and watch them disappear off the map for good! Oh, and remember – don't open the Loot Chest otherwise it runs the sneak attack! ●

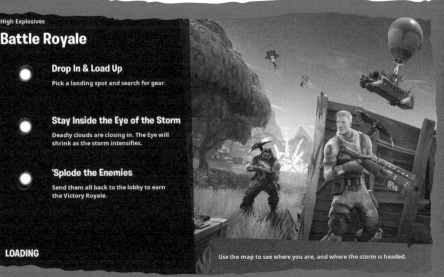

High Explosives

Battle Royale

Drop In & Load Up
Pick a landing spot and search for gear.

Stay Inside the Eye of the Storm
Deadly clouds are closing in. The Eye will shrink as the storm intensifies.

'Splode the Enemies
Send them all back to the lobby to earn the Victory Royale.

LOADING

Use the map to see where you are, and where the storm is headed.

MAP MADNESS

The Fortnite map is without doubt one of the most constantly evolving game worlds in the history of videogames. Epic Games is constantly looking for new and inventive ways to keep things fresh not just in terms of gameplay, but in how it reshapes huge chunks of the Fortnite Island map that players spend so much time on. Let's take a look at some of the most recent changes to the battlefield!

Loot Lake

Loot Lake has gone through quite a lot of changes since Fortnite Battle Royale began. First Kevin the Cube arrived, turning the water purple. Then there was the floating island high above it, and more recently it's been transformed into a Stonehenge-esque type location with lots of flowers and mini islands surrounding it.

Haunted Castle

Haunted Hills has always been quite the spooky location to drop into during a match, but it became even more frightening when Epic Games decided to drop a Haunted Castle into the mix! Explore it and you'll find a handful of Loot Chests, as well as creepy coffins! But don't blame us if you get scared, Fortnite Fans!

Frosty Flights

Looking for an X-4 Stormwing Plane to take to the skies in? Then drop into Frosty Flights, which first appeared at the start of Season 7 of Fortnite Battle Royale. Located in the south-western corner of the map, Frosty Flights is loaded with loot, plane hangars, houses and zip lines that lead to the chilly Polar Peak.

Polar Peak

Polar Peak can be found nestled in the centre of the winter wonderland that arrived during Season 7 of Fortnite Battle Royale. At the time of going to press it was the highest place on the Fortnite map. It's a cool place to venture to and soak up the snowy sight if you have some downtime in the multiplayer match.

Happy Hamlet

If you feel like taking a break from blasting opponents and fancy a little sight-seeing get yourself to the southern edge of the map to the west of Lucky Landing. There you'll find Happy Hamlet, a tiny, weeny European styled town. This place used to be Flush Factory, a serious drop-in hot spot for players!

Flush Factory

If you go looking for Flush Factory right now chances are you probably won't find it, because at the time of going to press the entire place was buried in snow. All that remains are the tips of buildings barely jutting out from underneath the white stuff. Next to it you'll find Happy Hamlet, which has replaced the rest of the area.

Frozen Lake

Remember Greasy Grove, the suburban neighbourhood over on the west side of the map? Well it's not there anymore, and instead there remains a huge frozen lake into which the buildings that once stood there have sunk. If you feel like it you can go for a quick skate around some of the old locations from days gone by.

DANCE OFF!

EMOTE ON **DANCE FLOORS** TO CAPTU[R]
THEM FOR YOUR TEAM!

DISCO, DISCO, DISCO!

Boogie all night long on the battlefield in the Limited Time Mode, **Disco Domination.**

Arguably one of the most intriguing – and hilarious – Limited Time Modes to hit Fortnite Battle Royale since it's inception is Disco Domination. The mode is essentially a boogie-skewered take on the classic Domination modes that have appeared in the likes of Call of Duty and Battlefield games over the years.

How it works in Epic Games' version is quite simple: dance floors pop up all over the map, which you then travel to and clear off any other players. Once the coast is clear start dancing. Dance long enough and you'll capture the dance floor. Capture enough dance floors and fill your team's dance bar to 100 and you win!

THE **ENEMY** HAS TAKEN OVER ONE OF YOUR *DANCE FLOORS*!

Crash The Party

Now, if you're not the one doing the dancing and a rival team has already started boogying hard you might want to play it smart before diving in headfirst. If you have a scoped gun, pick a few enemies off from a distance. If you've rockets, send a few 'em their way to thin out the crowds, and then rush in there with your squad for the win.

Team Dance Off

The way Disco Domination works in terms of teams is by splitting up 100 players into two groups of 50, so you really need to work together with your squad mates to capture the dance floors and eliminate opposing players. Unlike in standard Battle Royale matches respawn is available during the Limited Time Mode, until the third and final Storm Eye has taken hold of the map, so keep an eye on it.

Loop It

While there are numerous dancing emotes to choose from in the game, the best ones to pick during Disco Domination are the ones that loop. Looping animations save you the hassle of opening the menu to keep repeating the same dance moves over and over until the dance floor has been captured.

Protect The Dance Floor

It's worth noting that you can't actually build on the dance floor when trying to take control of it, but what you can – and absolutely should – do is build some sort of protection around the area to avoid being picked off from a distance by a handful of opposing players brandishing high-powered sniper rifles. A good way to capture a dance floor quickly is to assign a teammate to building duties, while the rest of the squad dances to snag it.

THIS IS A STICK UP!

Hints and tips for mastering the Grappler in Fortnite Battle Royale.

Fortnite Battle Royale is already so much fun to play, but do you know what makes it even more ridiculously enjoyable? The addition of The Grappler - a nifty new gadget that has opened up a whole new world of traversal opportunities in skirmishes! Essentially, this thing turns your character into Spider-Man thanks to its abilities. It also changes the dynamic of battle big time – nowhere is safe now!

What is it?

The Grappler is a plunger that can be shot at any surface in the game world. Once it connects with the surface it yanks you towards the target area. It's essentially like having Spider-Man's web-shooting ability in Fortnite Battle Royale, and so much fun to play with.

M Is For Momentum

Shortly after The Grappler arrived Epic Games added a little something extra to its abilities with the momentum function. Now when firing it at a moving vehicle or another player you are rewarded with a speed boost as you hurtle towards them.

Limited Range

It's important to remember that range is limited when using The Grappler – it is just a length of rope tied to a plunger after all! It's easy to spot when not in range too – the target reticule will appear as an X.

Fast Mover

The Grappler has 15 shots in total, so you can move around super fast in certain situations once it's in your arsenal, but don't forget to keep an eye on how many you have left otherwise you could wind up staring down the sights of a gun.

Rush Mode

If you come across an enemy and they start blasting at you use The Grappler to zip towards them super quickly. This usually causes them to get disorientated, giving you enough time to switch to a weapon, take them out and grab a kill.

A Quick Escape

Sometimes things can get frantic in Fortnite Battle Royale, so having The Grappler to hand can be extremely useful in situations like these. If you're running low on health and someone is attacking just use it to flee the scene!

Height Advantage

Gaining a height advantage is essential to survival in Fortnite Battle Royale, and while building structures are key to this, so is The Grappler. If you need to check out an area from a vantage point use it to zip up a structure and scope the area.

Stealth Attack

If you spot an opponent high up on a structure picking off enemies from a distance use The Grappler to zip up to their location quietly while they're distracted and then take them out from behind with your weapon of choice!

Combo Attacks

The Grappler is excellent for pulling off killer combo attacks on enemies. To perform one of these you'll need a close range weapon in your arsenal, such as a shotgun. Simply zip to their location and blast them up close with your gun.

FORTNITE EVENTS

Take a deep dive into Fortnite Battle Royale's tournament system!

When Patch 6.10. for Fortnite Battle Royale hit gaming platforms it brought with it one of the most exciting new features of the game – Tournaments! These Events allowed gamers the world over to compete alongside and against some of the best Fortnite Battle Royale players. It was a huge moment for Fortnite, so let's take a look at some of the Events that took place over the last twelve months.

Practice Tournament Solo

The first Event to launch with the new game mode was a solo Event requiring players to score six points every match by taking out enemies. Players that nabbed a minimum of 20 points were rewarded with a pin.

Friday Night Fortnite

Friday Night Fortnite was a super fast and hectic squad-based mode that charged teams with scoring up to six points in a match, and earning at least 25 during a team session. Like the previous mode the reward was a cool in-game pin!

Practice Tournament Duos

This Duos Mode asked players to grab a gaming buddy and lead the charge against the rest of the world's Fortnite Battle Royale players by scoring 20 points minimum in exchange for another in-game pin over the course of three days.

Scavenger Pop-Up Cup Duos

The arrival of Scavenger Pop-Up Cup brought with it some cool treats for Fortnite Battle Royale fans. This tournament allowed Epic Games to test some new gameplay tweaks, including reduced materials and storm circle adjustments.

Winter Royale

The Winter Royale was without doubt the biggest Fortnite Battle Royale tournament to launch with the arrival of Events. Why? Players were competing to win one million dollars worth of prizes! Crazy stuff, right?!

Alchemist Pop-Up Cup Solo

The Alchemist Pop-Up Cup brought with it numerous gameplay adjustments to make the matches more interesting, as well as testing Limited Time Modes. The aim for players was to grab at least 20 points during the tournament for a pin.

GET CREATIVE!

Everything you need to know about Fortnite Battle Royale's **Creative Mode!**

Fortnite: Creative is probably one of the biggest and most interesting features ever to grace the world of Fortnite Battle Royale. What is it? We're glad you asked! Fortnite: Creative came with the arrival of Season 7 and is essentially a huge sandbox mode that allows you to create your own private island.

Yeah, it's awesome. In it you'll be able to invite your friends to play around and have as much fun as you want without worrying about other players trying to blast you back to the Start Menu. You can design everything from games, races, challenges and matches where you and your pals can duke it out against each other.

Let's take a look at how exactly Fortnite: Creative works!

Player Islands

Player Islands are essentially blank slates for you to create stuff on from scratch. These creative spaces act like standalone servers and stay active for up to four hours at a time. You're allotted four islands, which allow you to mess around with different kinds of designs so that you can find one that works best for you.

My Island Menu

The My Island Menu is really useful. To access it all you have to do is open up the Main Menu while you're messing around on your own personal island. Then simply look for the Game Tab, which will allow you to stop and start any crazy games you come up with or revert the island back to it's original game state.

make A movie

The Replay function is one of the things we imagine Fortnite fans are going to have an absolute ball with in Fortnite: Creative. When playing in this unique mode the servers that host your island remain live for four hours, but what's really interesting is that all of your actions are recorded in 30-minute chunks and saved, so that if you pulled off an awesome stunt or takedown you can re-watch it!

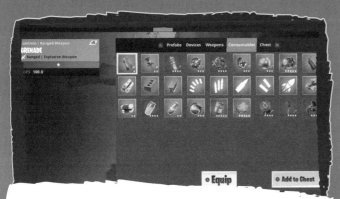

Inventory Creation

The Creative Inventory is easily accessed from the Inventory Menu and lets you spawn everything from buildings to weaponry and in-game consumables. Heck, you can even craft Loot Chests and Loot Llamas and fill them with whatever you want! And because of this you can either be extremely generous or really tight with Loot and items to make matches easier or harder depending on play styles.

Prefabs

Prefabs are pre-existing structures and will save you a whole heap of time. This menu is insanely big. There are so many structures for you to choose from to drop around the island, including chunks of Tilted Towers and some smaller less recognizable buildings. You can also add furniture, including fridges and shelves to buildings, so feel free to pack each to the gills with items for harvesting in fights.

Let's Fly

Did we mention you are also able to fly in Fortnite: Creative? Well now you know! Flying allows you to move around the map at speed. It also helps when you want to build structures on different sections of the island at speed, but you can also whizz through the air during any battles you create and even shoot your opponents, which makes for some crazy fire-fight dynamics!

Memory Cap

This is one of the most important things to remember when playing around in Fortnite: Creative. The Memory Usage feature is Epic Games' attempt to stop servers being overloaded and crashing. The more players that jump into the world of Fortnite: Creative the less memory becomes available. At the time of going to press the Memory Usage is indicated by a bar at the bottom of the screen, so be sure to keep an eye out when playing with your Fortnite friends.

FOOD FIGHT

The fast food war to end all fast food wars comes to Fortnite Battle Royale!

Food Fight is without doubt one of the most popular Limited Time Modes to come to Fortnite Battle Royale since the game launched back in 2017. It pits two teams of 12 players against each other with both teams starting off on opposite sides of a huge wall that lowers after the countdown clock projected onto it reaches zero.

Tomato Heads

The twist is it's not just a race to eliminate the opposition, it's got a story too. The mode pits teams from rival fast food chains in the Fortnite universe against each other – namely Durr Burger and Pizza Pit. Players on the Durr Burger side have heads shaped like – you guessed it – hamburgers, while Pizza Pit warriors run around the map with Tomato Head, um, heads! It's crazy fun! Each team has to protect their mascot, so the trick is to use the ticking clock at

Our mascot's health is at 10 percent!

the outset of a match to build as much protection around it as quickly as possible.

Build Big

While the temptation may be to just grab as much loot as you can at the outset of a match, this is definitely the wrong approach. During our time on it we saw teams craft the most amazingly elaborate forts around mascots that boggled the mind. Loot is easy to come by in this mode, so don't fret. Always stay close to your team's fort and any time it looks like it's getting damaged start building extra defences around it, or you risk losing the

match if the mascot's health reaches zero.

Respawn

If you get killed during the match in Food Fight Limited Time Mode don't worry, like regular multiplayer modes in other videogames you'll respawn on the map a few seconds later to

re-join the fight. In fact, dying in a match isn't a bad thing at all – if you're smart you can glide all the way into a team's fort and hit them with a surprise attack. But chances are you'll get taken out by an opponent while doing it, so make sure you dole out as much damage as possible with the time you have.

It's Been Coming

Epic Games had been teasing this fantastic food themed mode for some time in the run up to release in late 2018 with a slew of fun things, including Twitter polls and tweaks to the game world map, including two rival food trucks parked next to each other, so this restaurant showdown was clearly something the team had been planning for some time. Like all Limited Time Modes it appeared only for a short stint before disappearing, so here's hoping we see Food Fight again soon! ●

STAY AFLOAT!

Fortnite Battle Royale's Glider Redeploy feature explained!

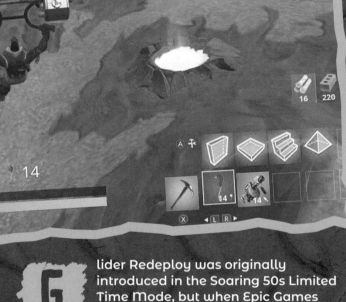

Glider Redeploy was originally introduced in the Soaring 50s Limited Time Mode, but when Epic Games decided to weave it into the main Battle Royale in 2018 it caused all sorts of problems for the team. Let's take a look at how it worked, what happened to it and how it now features in the game at the time of writing.

Basically it allows you to leap off a surface at a height and deploy the glider to stop you crashing to the ground. It was such a success the team opted to include it in all Battle Royale modes.

Bad Plan

However, the new feature didn't exactly go down well with players in the game. Sure, it was a whole lot of fun but many players felt that it upset the balance of the game, in particular during Solo, Duos and Squad Game Modes. You see the original idea behind the Glider Redeploy was to

that the team left it in the game untouched? Either way, Epic Games felt it was best to remove it, so they shelved the ability with the release of Patch 6.3.0. At the time of writing it was still functioning in Playground Mode and other Limited Time Modes.

Despite the fact the ability wasn't working in the main game modes, many believe it will be making a return in some form or another in the future. Until then you can still enjoy using it in any of the supported Limited Time Modes it's included in. ●

allow for better mobility during combat in matches while creating loads of interesting new situations on the battlefield.

That plan backfired because players kept using it to flee from fire-fights. It meant players were losing out on kills and getting frustrated with opponents bailing off a building or a cliff edge at the first sign of trouble. With that, the developers decided to pull it, saying in a blog post "We did not live up to expectations of quickly iterating on the mechanic and communicating plans."

Gone, Not Forgotten

What did you think Fortnite fans? Did you agree with the removal, or would you have preferred

TOYS, TOYS TOYS!

Fortnite fever has well and truly taken hold of the world with the arrival of a slew of collectible action figures, key chains and figurines from some of the world's biggest toy companies, including Funko and McFarlane, the people behind a bunch of highly sought after action figure ranges from the likes of The Walking Dead, Halo and Epic Games' Gears of War. But be warned Fortnite fans - if you want to add them all to your shelves you're going to need really deep pockets...and lots of space!

Some of the most popular collectors items right now are Funko's Pop! Vinyl series. The company has teamed up with Epic Games to release a whole heap of figures based on the game, each one awesomely replicated from the games' 3D modelling. Check 'em all out here and start adding them to your wish lists right now!

5 STAR: FORTNITE

5 star toys for 5 star fans!

TomatoHead

TomatoHead is part of the 5 Star: Fortnite Series 1 collection, and is bound to become something of a collector's item when stocks of this one run dry. TomatoHead first appeared back in April of 2018 as part of Season 4 and quickly became a fan favourite, re-appearing again in Season 5 and 6.

Love Ranger

Who wouldn't want this cute and deadly Love Ranger in their collection? With its huge head, concrete-like skin, stone wings and the super rare Tat Axe Pickaxe, it's both cuddly and terrifying in equal measure. The Love Ranger also comes with an explosive surprise for your friends – the Impulse Grenade! How sweet!

Omega

Of all of the 5 Star: Fortnite range this one is arguably the coolest looking. Omega comes kitted out in full body armour like some sort of comic book super villain. He's clad in a pitch-black skin-suit with terrifying red eyes and the groovy sticky grenade. Add this one to your collection and you'll be the envy of all your friends!

Moonwalker

Released as part of the Space Explorer skin set during Season 3 of Fortnite Battle Royale the Moonwalker 5 Star: Fortnite figure comes clad in a cosy space suit with open helmet showing off the character's face. It also features an EVA Harvesting Tool as well as a small serving of Slurp Juice.

Zoey

Say hello to Zoey, the funky-looking star of Season 4 Sweet Tooth set. Clad in pink top, black leggings with white stripes and her super slick pink nightcap, Zoey is definitely one of the most colourful characters in the 5 Star: Fortnite range. She comes holding the Lollipopper Harvesting Tool and a set of bandages.

POP VINYL!

Big heads for big fans!

Highrise Assault Trooper

First up in the Pop Vinyl! Series is the Highrise Assault Trooper, a familiar face to fans of the game and a regular on the Fortnite Shop homepage. This guy may not be as rare as the Black Knight, or as awesome as Omega, but we still think he's awesome.

Rex

Roar! Say hello to our little friend, Rex! Part of the Dino Guard set released back in March 2018, this Legendary skin can now be yours in toy form complete with orange bandana and gnarly teeth guaranteed to scare off the other toys as well as the competition. Watch out though, because this one bites!

Dark Voyager

Part of the Space Explorers set that first appeared back in Season 3, the Dark Voyager was a Legendary outfit jazzed up with an orange vest pattern and pitch-black astronaut helmet. Now that it's been made into a Pop! Figure we're pretty sure this one is going to look absolutely amazing on your toy shelf!

Red Nosed Raider

Celebrate Christmas all year round with this awesome holiday themed Pop Vinyl! figure. Replicated exactly as it is in the game, the Red Nosed Raider comes clad in a long-sleeve jumper, red pants and sports a red nose and antlers. Ho-Ho-Ho!

Merry Marauder

Hands up out there anyone who was terrified at the sight of this angry gingerbread man coming running towards you with an assault rifle? Scary right? Well, it seems Pop Vinyl! knew this and transformed the gun-toting terror into a collectible figure! The Marauder would look much cuter if he just learned to smile, right?

PLASTIC FANTASTIC!

Check out the first series of McFarlane Fortnite figures!

Skull Trooper

Everyone loves Skull Trooper, so it's no surprise that McFarlane has decided to immortalize the skin in action figure form. This demented and bone-chilling figure comes packed with a slew of cool items, including Sharp Precision Back Bling, Legendary Bolt-Action Sniper Rifle and the Death Valley Pickaxe. Grab this one before it sells out, folks!

Cuddle Team Leader

Pink fur fans rejoice it's the Cuddle Team Leader! When your friends see this they'll laugh, they'll ogle and probably scream with terror remembering that time you wiped them out using this skin. The figure comes with the Cuddle Bow Back Bling, Legendary Scar Assault Rifle and the Rainbow Smash Pickaxe. Own it!

Black Knight

Whoa! We absolutely love this Black Knight figure from McFarlane! It's no surprise that he was chosen to appear in the first wave of toys; it is one of the rarest character skins in the game. The Black Knight comes complete with Black Shield Back Bling, Grenade Launcher, and the terrifying Axecalibur Harvesting tool.

Rainbow Smash

Essential for all unicorn lovers, this Rainbow Smash replica prop is a whopping 39 inches long, which means it's perfect for fans of Fortnite Cosplay, or those who like to smash their way to victory. With spinning wheels, wild colours and absolutely amazing craftsmanship on behalf of McFarlane this is a must-own!

Raptor

This Raptor figure is sculpted and painted from in-game assets, and comes complete with the mighty Drum Gun, as well as the Icebreaker Pickaxe. Standing at 7 inches tall and billed as the Swiss Army knife of Fortnite Battle Royale character skins, Raptor is guaranteed to look the part on your Fortnite collectible shelf.

PINT-SIZED HEROES

Teeny, tiny two-man squads!

Omega & Valor

Add some pint-sized power to your collection with these two miniscule figures from Funko. Sure, they're small but that doesn't mean that they won't have your back in battle!

Rex & Tricera Ops

These miniaturised versions of Rex and Tricera Ops are so cool we want them in our collection right now! Pop these two next to your Rex Pop Vinyl! figure.

Skull Trooper & Ghoul Trooper

Spook up your collection of Fortnite figures with this double pack that includes Skull Trooper and Ghoul Trooper Pint-sized Heroes. They're teeny, tiny and really, really terrifying!

Black Knight & Red Knight

The Black Knight makes another appearance in our toy round up, this time alongside the Red Knight and in pint-sized form. Grab this double-act before they disappear off shelves forever!

MONOPOLY: FORTNITE EDITION

◆ Fast-Dealing Property Trading Game ◆

MONOPOLY

®BRAND

FORTNITE

BATTLE YOUR OPPONENTS, AND AVOID THE STORM!

E6603
AGES 13+
2-7 PLAYERS

Hasbro Gaming

The world's most famous videogame meets the world's most famous board game!

Holy Moly Fortnite fans! It's the Monopoly: Fortnite Edition, a super addictive board game spin on the most famous videogame in the world.

With gameplay, design and components directly inspired by gameplay mechanics, including map locations and loot chest cards, this is a must-have for any fans of both Fortnite Battle Royale and Fortnite Save The World.

The game comes jam-packed with cool stuff, including 27 character outfit cards that take the form of cardboard outfits with pawn stands, 15 Storm cards, 16 Location cards, 16 loot chest cards, 8 Wall cards, a guide booklet and 110 Health Point Chips, which replace the classic Monopoly money synonymous with the original game.

Once you've chosen your character it's time to throw the die and start the game. This then allows you to pick up health packs, craft walls and dole out damage to other players sitting around the board competing against you.

Monopoly: Fortnite Edition can be played by two to seven players, and is aimed at anyone aged 13 years old and up, so any of our younger readers out there might need to check with their parents before picking up a copy of this one. ●

NERFED

Lock n' load with the Nerf AR-L Blaster!

If playing Fortnite on your console, PC or phone wasn't enough then you'll be super excited to know that you'll be able to play Fortnite for real (kind of) come June 2019 when Nerf's AR-L Blaster replica gun arrives on store shelves.

The stylish plastic rifle features a 10-dart magazine and requires four AA batteries. Now, before you start freaking out the darts are made of foam, so getting hit with one won't leave any marks, but just remember if you do pick this one up and decided to recreate classic battles from the game never aim for someone's face!

At the moment this is currently the only Nerf gun replica created by the toy maker and Epic Games, but don't be surprised if we see more announced in the run up to, and after the initial release of the AR-L Blaster. ●

FORTNITE

FORTNITE BATTLE ROYALE